I0187735

A Clear And Compelling Dream

How To Harness The Power Of Your Big Dream

Dr Michael Pierquet

Blue Diamond Marketing LLC

GREEN BAY, WI

Copyright © 2018 by **Michael J Pierquet**

All rights reserved. No part of this publication may be reproduced, distributed or transmitted in any form or by any means, (electronic, mechanical, photocopying, recording, or otherwise) prior written permission of the author and publisher of this book.

The scanning, uploading, and distribution of this book via the internet or via any other means without the permission of the publisher is illegal and punishable by law.

Michael J Pierquet/Blue Diamond Marketing LLC
PO Box 658
Sister Bay, WI 54234
www.mikepierquet.com

Publisher's Note: This is a work of fiction. Names, characters, places, and incidents are a product of the author's imagination. Any resemblance to actual people, living or dead, or to businesses, companies, events, institutions, or locales is completely coincidental.

A Clear And Compelling Dream/ Michael Pierquet. -- 1st ed.
ISBN 978-0-9827937-1-8

CONTENTS

Definitions

Clear:

Leaving no doubt; obvious or unambiguous; having or feeling no doubt or confusion.

Compelling:

Evoking interest, attention, or admiration in a powerfully irresistible way; not able to be refuted; inspiring conviction; not able to be resisted.

Dream:

A cherished aspiration, ambition, or ideal; a thing perceived as wonderful or perfect.

Forward

It has been said that there are two kinds of simplicity; one that lives on this side of complexity, the other on the far side.

I hope this book is a pleasant step on your path to the life you want and deserve, and that it helps you transcend the complexity in your life to find some simplicity on the other side.

Such was the path of this book. It started with simple ideas that grew suddenly too long and complex, and not at all how the book wanted to be. So began the process of rewriting, refining, distillation, and trying to return to simplicity again - but this time on the other side of the complexity.

It turns out that writing a short book is not easier than writing a long book. Boiling ideas down to their essence without losing the flavor of what they are is tricky.

Every cut passage cried out for mercy, but in the quest for simplicity, none was granted. The lost passages will arise again in another work. But not here.

This work is meant to provide a simple framework that can be read quickly and effortlessly. It's purpose is to help you see yourself and your world just a bit differently, and hopefully inspire you to think about creating a different kind of life - the one you've always wanted.

If what you read here resonates, and you would like another step, I created some bonuses that you can find at **mikepierquet.com/book-bonus.**

If you would like to come play and evolve with us, I invite you to my website at **MikePierquet.com**.

Michael Pierquet

Someday Island

Loved ones can change your life in unexpected ways.

Eric was a once in a lifetime kind of friend, and for more than 20 years we were close like brothers.

Every year without fail we did the Canada fishing trip, the Montana trip, the fall camping trip, and the winter cruise. There were endless family outings, dinners out, and work projects.

For a stretch there, Eric went through a lot - parents died, job of 20 years gone, divorce. Through it all we remained good friends, and being the person he was, he came out the other side doing OK.

After the divorce, Eric was still part of our family, so when I got the text that said "what up tonight," I told him, and that's how we all ended up at our favorite restaurant. It was a wonderful evening full of friends, family, fun, laughter.

At the end there was only Eric and I, and we accidentally took a little mental trip to Someday Isle. Ever been there? It goes like this: *Someday I'll* do this. *Someday I'll* do that. Yup, and then I'm gonna do this, and this, and that. You bet.

For Eric, he was going to finish out his commitment to the desk job he had taken, then go back to the job he had always loved. Maybe move back to Green Bay, or perhaps Montana. He vowed to never again miss the Canada trip like he had the last one.

We dreamed and schemed and finally left late in the night, satisfied with our smart talk and brimming with optimism about all the things we were going to do, and all the changes we were going to make... someday.

In the parking lot, I teased Eric about how he ended up with the truck I had wanted to buy. In my best smart ass voice I said, "I hope you know you're driving away in my truck." With a laugh and a wave he was off, while I tended to phone messages.

That was the last time I ever saw Eric.

Because on the way home he died.

When you are standing the day after an accident with your heart in your throat, staring at the tire ruts in the grass, the pieces of truck strewn about, the small mementos of a person's life scattered along the path as the vehicle rolled - the baseball cap, a bottle of water, the flashlight pen our friend Tom gave us in Canada... that's when you know your life will never be the same.

That's when it hits you hard that everything you ever did, or were ever going to do, can be gone in an instant.

And you wonder... if you were gone in an instant, did it even matter that you were here?

You search for meaning in tragic death. You search for why. You search for reasons... but I couldn't find any. All I could find was the thought that I couldn't let Eric's death be for no reason. I just couldn't.

Our last talk was all about our "someday plans", and that conversation rang on in my head because the hard, bitter truth is that most of the things I said are the same damn things I've been telling myself my whole life.

In my quiet, tortured moments my inner voice began asking too many questions. Does it make any difference that you are here? Do you even matter? Are you doing what you are supposed to be doing? And how could I possibly answer yes, when I had the conversation with Eric in my head to prove otherwise.

Then the voice took to telling rather than asking: "To whom much is given, much is expected - you are not living a big enough life."

Over and over the words came whenever they felt like it - strong, insistent, and seemingly from somewhere outside of myself.

These were not words I could ignore, because they sounded true. I have been given gifts, yet I was spending my life doing small things. My intellect tried hard to logically argue otherwise, but always the voice countered with… to whom much is given, much is expected…

These were the thoughts and questions that melded into my intense sadness and pain, and changed something in me. I could no longer go on thinking and talking about who I always wanted to be. I had to start being who I always wanted to be.

I don't know why Eric died. I only know that I vowed I would make something good come from it. And that something was the inspiration for me to do what I told him I was going to do on his last night on earth.

And so I made a right turn in life. I sold my business of 30 years and headed down a totally different path. This book is one of the results of that right turn.

I hope it matters.

Thanks Eric.

CHAPTER ONE

Deathbed Regrets

Maybe you will die like this...

One final trip to hear the doctor say, "I'm sorry, there is nothing more to be done, this is the end for you." You knew it was coming, still the inevitability and disbelief punch you in the gut.

Your life is over.

Everything seems different on the drive home. Two people laugh on the sidewalk. How strange it seems that they laugh while you die. Others are somber, worried, rushing to their next task. You want to scream out the window, "WAKE UP! You don't have time for this!"

Back home you sit quietly alone on the patio, watching the giant fluffy clouds playing against the blue sky. A light coolness in the air makes the sunlight feel warm and tingly on your face. Pretty birds fuss at the feeder, and the faint sound of a lawn mower brings you the sweet smell of freshly cut grass. It is all so beautiful, and you sit a long time - thinking.

Back in the house you see the years of hard work, the remodeling, the new addition - bittersweet memories. You stare at the pictures on your mantle and think about the fun and pain, the squabbles and fights, the laughter and happy times, the people you've known and loved, the things you did, the things you always meant to do.

That's when it hits you... this is judgement day. It is time for your quiet moment of truth. This is the day you decide whether or not you lived the life you always intended to live. Your friends, your family, the newspaper, the TV, your priest, cannot help you now.

It's your turn.

On the last day there is nothing to be done about a life gone by. Token I love you's will not change a lifetime of silence. Token I'm sorry's will not change how you treated people. Wishing things had gone differently is hopeless.

On your last day it's too late...

But right now it isn't. Right now you have the power to make sure that your last day comes with contentment, fulfillment, peace, and a feeling that you lived fully and with gusto. Right now you have the power to make sure that your life matters.

You will have a final day on earth. Maybe you will see it coming, maybe not. You can't stop it, but you can make that day a good one... possibly even the best one.

When you make choices going forward based on how you want to feel on your last day, then you can live, and die, in peace.

There is nothing worse for a soul to endure than deathbed regrets.

Don't be there.

CHAPTER TWO

Swimming Downstream

Did you ever swim in a river?

Imagine... that you are standing alone on the river's edge. A morning mist hangs lightly over the water as you watch the slow, relentless, powerful current flow gently over and around the boulders in its path. All is quiet and peaceful as you step gingerly into the cool dark water, and feel your toes sink into the silty bottom.

One step and then another, deeper and deeper, and with each step the current pulls more powerfully at your legs, until finally your feet lose touch with the bottom. It's time to swim.

At first you swim against the current, holding your position. With more effort you move slowly upstream, but each stroke becomes more difficult as the pain builds in your arms and shoulders, and the relentless current works tirelessly to push you downstream.

You could be in top physical condition. You could be stubborn, exert tremendous willpower, use positive affirmations - I know I can! I know I can! You could take performance enhancing drugs, or drugs to kill the pain. You could hire a group of Olympic swimmers to coach you and even swim alongside, shouting encouragement all the while.

You could try anything you want, but guess what? Sooner or later, one way or another, bruised, battered, and beaten, you *are* going downstream my friend - even if it's underwater.

Swimming upstream is a game you can't win.

And if you turn and swim with the current? Easy, fun, effortless. Same river, different result. The river hasn't changed, you have. You've aligned with its power instead of fighting against it.

The universe around you is like that river - flowing with relentless power, always moving, always changing, yet always the same. The water you see now is miles downstream by nightfall, yet water is still there.

The river and the universe it lives in operate according to timeless and unchanging natural laws, some of which are visible to you and some that are not.

You don't see evaporation, but you know when it rains on your head. You don't see gravity, yet you wouldn't jump off a building and hope it's not there.

Gravity is invisible but real. It is an unchangeable law of nature.

So too there are natural laws and principles in the invisible world of thought. They are often less apparent than the physical laws we see, but just as real as gravity.

You can learn these principles and flow with them, or you can struggle against them. You can spend your life kicking and screaming, complaining about injustices, and believing the world is unfair. Or not.

You can swim upstream or down.

CHAPTER THREE

Software Update

Why are you who you are?

You are who you are because of the thoughts you have. You are a being made up of thoughts, and your life is the collective sum of those thoughts.

Happiness is a thought about how good your life is. Your desires are thoughts about what you want. Your values are thoughts about what is important. Success is what you think it is. Your relationships are thoughts about other people. Your emotions are thoughts about how you feel. Your past exists only in the thoughts you have about it.

The critical question then, is why do you have the thoughts you have? Let's think about that using a computer analogy.

A computer consists of hardware and software. Hardware is the collection of mechanical parts that form the physical structure of the computer, and software is the collective of programs that run the hardware. The software brings the hardware to life.

The primary software that controls everything is the Mac or Windows operating system you see when you turn your computer on. There are other software programs as well, some of which you see, and some that run silently and invisibly in the background.

Each software came about because a computer company spent huge sums of money and many years of effort to create it. They followed up with more years of redesigning, upgrading, removing glitches, and fine tuning. Safeguards were placed to stop viruses and malware from being imbedded without your knowledge or consent, and strict guidelines were followed to ensure that each software plays well with the others.

They did all of this because if any software is not compatible, or has bugs, glitches, or viruses, then things go bad.

You've got a computer on your shoulders too. Your physical brain is your hardware, and your software is the thoughts, beliefs, and emotions that run your brain. Your collective software is what we might call your mind.

Your brain is more complex than any computer, but let me ask you something. Who created the software running your mind and your life? Who programmed *your* operating system?

Did a crack team of computer geeks work for many years to create and perfect your programming? Did they follow up to fix the glitches and remove the viruses and malware that infected you along the way? Did they make sure all your software is compatible? That didn't happen, did it.

Instead your mind was programmed for you by all the influences in your life since you were born.

Your parents were the major programmers, followed by siblings, teachers, classmates, and books. Television shows, advertisements, Gilligan, the Skipper, the Marlboro man, friends, lovers, professors, spouses, priests, and things that just happened to you along the way, have all taken their turn at programming the thoughts and beliefs into your mind that now influence who you are, what you believe, how you think, what you do, and what you have.

As a child, you had little say so over what you were taught to believe. When your parents told you the rich neighbor was a jerk - just like all the other rich people, you didn't come back with, "you know what mom, I don't think that belief is going to help me later on in life, so I choose not to believe that rich people are jerks." No, you sucked it in like a sponge because that's the only thing a child can do, and that's when your belief system about money was born.

As an adult, you have no doubt tried to confront childhood beliefs and create your own - probably with varying degrees of success. Good for you.

If you have not, that is understandable too. It's easy to drift merrily or not so merrily through life, blissfully or not so blissfully unaware that thoughts, feelings, and life don't just happen to you by accident. These things are determined by the visible and invisible software.

If you don't know about the software, then life just sort of happens to you. But once you know, you get to decide if life will happen to you, or if you will happen to it.

The software runs automatically in the background all the time, monitoring you and influencing your interactions with the world around you. It largely determines what you perceive to be true, and if you accept these perceptions as truth, they in turn reinforce and strengthen your programming - whether that programming is correct or not.

This happens because the software influences what your mind's eye sees. You see what you believe. If your software tells you there is a lack of abundance in the world, you see examples of scarcity all around you. If it tells you people are inherently bad, you focus on bad things people do, and look for badness in people you meet. If you believe people are untrustworthy, you see untrustworthiness.

These things you see support and justify the programming that caused you to see them in the first place. If you think wealthy people are bad, you notice examples of that, and when you do, the software says, "see, I was right, wealth is bad." This makes it easier for you to see still more examples, which in turn ingrain that belief deeper into your psyche.

On the other hand, if you think wealthy people are good, you will see that, and every time you do, that belief is reinforced.

Your programming influences what you see, what you see influences your programming, and they feed upon each other.

To you, the things you see are not perceptions, but rather the truth, and you take actions and make choices accordingly. You view other people without that "truth" as wrong. You surround yourself with people of similar beliefs because you feel compatible. You get each other. You like each other. You make sense to one another. You are proud to stand together against the unenlightened who don't yet realize that you are right.

This is how deep, self-propagating beliefs are created. This is how the software takes seeds that were planted in childhood and eventually grows you a garden of vegetables that you may or may not like.

Most of your beliefs were learned from your parents and other people during periods of your life when you were susceptible to influence. The beliefs you learned along the way tend to keep you on a certain path, sometimes all the way to death.

That's because these beliefs act like an internal thermostat that regulates the conditions of your life, much the way the thermostat in your house regulates the temperature.

Your internal thermostat is set at the level determined by your beliefs, and the software works tirelessly and fiercely to keep your life at that level. If you venture too far in any direction from the thermostat setting, the software will do it's best to bring you back to what you really believe.

That's how a wealthy person can lose all their money, and in short order get back to where they were. That is also how a poor person can win the lottery, and then quickly get back to being poor. It's why when extra money comes unexpectedly into your life, you spend it. It's also why you work hard to finally pay off that car, and then promptly buy another one with a similar payment. This is how you escape one abusive relationship, only to find another.

If your house thermostat is set at 60 degrees, you wouldn't expect a temperature other than that. Likewise don't expect your life circumstances to be different from where your internal thermostat is set.

If your wealth thermostat is set at poverty level, don't expect other than poverty. If your happiness thermostat is set at miserable, expect misery. If your relationship thermostat is set at the complaining and bickering level, you will have that. If your health thermostat is set at the couch potato, drink beer, and watch stupid TV shows level, don't wonder why your health fails.

The problem is that the sneaky software has been hiding the thermostat from you all these years and allowing your belief system to determine the default setting.

If you want a different level of success in your life, then you've got to reach in there, turn that thing up, and be ready to feel the wrath of the software when you do. Success requires that you stop being a victim of the thermostat, and start taking control.

Learning to understand and control your software is a critical undertaking because left alone, the software *will* grow a life for you. It just won't be the life you want and were supposed to have.

If you can accept that you have software programs running in your head - some that you can see, some that you can't, some that help you, some that hurt you, but all of which you have the power to change, then you are turning to swim with the flow.

You have the power to think about your thinking.

Do it.

CHAPTER FOUR

Icebergs

You think you have problems.

If you are typical, you want to fix those problems by taking actions to make them go away. For example, if you are overweight, you psyche yourself up, conjure up in your mind all the bad things that will happen if you don't change, use brute willpower, pass on the brownies at work, no more ice cream, and it's down to the gym every morning.

It seems so logical to want to change your circumstances by changing the behaviors and actions that caused them in the first place.

That's because we inherently know that results come from actions. We want the result of losing weight, so we exercise more. We want more money, so we save some every month. We want to attract a mate, so we buy new clothes. On and on it goes. The equation looks like this:

ACTIONS = RESULTS

While true, this equation is only the obvious tip of the iceberg you see sticking above the water. The underwater part you don't see is what determines the quality of life you will have.

The underwater part is your software. It is the thoughts and beliefs rolling around in your head that underly everything you do.

These may be conscious thoughts, or subconscious thoughts running silently in the background. They may be helpful beliefs that you created, or harmful beliefs placed there by your past. Either way, everything is in there, influencing you - all the time. The rest of the equation is this:

THOUGHTS = ACTIONS = RESULTS

This is the equation of life. This is some simplicity on the far side of complexity - yet the apparent simpleness belies the underlying power of the equation to transform your life, once you understand the nuances behind it.

Thoughts cause the actions that create the results. Without thoughts, actions can't happen. Without actions, there are no results.

The conditions and circumstances of your life right now are results generated by your previous thoughts and actions. Results can be in your outside world, in your mind, or both. Changing a thought is both an action and a result, which is why change can occur instantly in your mind, even though it might not be manifested in the physical world until later.

Except for accidents, genetic issues, or unavoidable health problems, everything you are and everything you have is a result of the things you did and didn't do so far. And you did or didn't do those things because of the thoughts you have. The thoughts you have are part of the software programming that's been going on from the day you were born right up to the time you are reading this sentence.

This is how your life right now is a *result* that came into being because of thoughts. You see then that if these thoughts were programmed into you randomly or accidentally based on your upbringing and your past, a life may have been created for you that is not really yours. Understanding the three parts of the equation and their relationship to each other is how you prevent that from happening in the future.

The three parts are intertwined and always will be. Your choice lies only in *how* they are intertwined. Look again at the equation and see that actions are the bridge between thoughts and results. Without actions nothing happens. Without actions dreams don't come true. You must take actions, but more than that, you must choose *why* you take them.

The why can be either of the other two parts of the equation - thoughts or results. Which of these you choose will have a profound impact on your life going forward.

For example, let's say you look in the mirror and see the result that you are overweight, so you stop eating donuts at work every morning. That is using a result (being overweight), to motivate your actions (stop eating donuts).

On the other hand, you may have the thought that you want to be healthy and live a long life, so you stop eating donuts. This is using a thought about what you want to motivate your actions.

Either way you stop eating donuts, but one motivation for doing so is based on a thought, and the other on a result. This is a critical distinction. One way is swimming upstream, the other down.

Prior to right now, you may not have been making a conscious choice about why you do what you do. You may not have even known there *was* a choice. If you are not aware of the equation, or the choice, then likely your life has been largely happening by accident.

For instance, let's say your childhood left you with the subconscious programming that marriage is bad, and that being fat is a way to keep the opposite sex away. Now you eat donuts because of thoughts you don't know you have, end up with results you don't want, and you don't know why.

If you do not grasp the whole equation, you do what most people do. You operate only in the superficial ACTIONS = RESULTS part of the equation. You see the result of being overweight and you take the action of dieting, without addressing the underlying thoughts that caused you to be overweight in the first place.

If you don't include thoughts in your equation, it's not because they aren't there, it's because you are blind to them. Thoughts are always part of the equation.

Unfortunately, these thoughts and beliefs are often operating below the surface, underwater, where you can't see them. In order to move your life forward in a coherent manner, you need awareness to bring them to the surface.

Once you find awareness, then you will see the insidious underside of operating your life based only on actions and results.

It starts innocently enough when you label certain results or circumstances in your life as "problems." When you see a result as a problem, the next logical step becomes doing something to make it go away.

Most likely you follow this script without conscious consideration or forethought, because that's how you've always done it, that's how everyone you know does it, and it's one of those things you do automatically. It's common sense, right? You have a problem, you put it on your list, and you fix it.

There is nothing inherently wrong with fixing problems. In fact, if you fixed your five biggest problems, you would probably feel much better about your life. But when you use problems as your source of motivation, and when you knowingly or unknowingly use the fixing of problems as a core strategy for improving your life, then you are expecting a deeply flawed structure to make your life better.

The flaw is that these problems are *current* circumstances created by *past* thoughts and actions - sometimes going all the way back to childhood. The problems you have now are a product of your past.

Thus, the problem fixing strategy forces you to spend your present and future life *reacting* to circumstances created by your past. It forces you to live REACTIVELY based on whatever problems you have at the moment.

And it's even worse than that, because often these problems are a result of software that was programmed into you without your input. Thus your life is being spent reacting to problems created by thoughts and beliefs that aren't even yours.

The question is, how can you move forward to create the life you want by reacting to conditions created by your past? The answer is of course, you can't. This orientation keeps you locked in a weird feedback loop wherein you are unknowingly allowing your past to dictate your future.

This is why using results to motivate actions is the tail wagging the dog.

On the flip side, when your actions are driven by *thoughts* about what you want, rather than as a reaction to *results* you see around you, then you are living PROACTIVELY. Now your actions are determined by your preferred future instead of your past. Thinking proactively is how you take your past out of the equation, and not have it predict or determine your future.

Being *proactive* is taking actions to create what you want. Being *reactive* is taking actions to make problems go away. These are profoundly different ways of operating your life.

Health is a good example. We call it a healthcare system, but it's really a disease care system designed to fix health problems that have already occurred. Cholesterol is up? Pop a pill. Blood pressure is up? Pop another pill.

Arteries are clogged? Let's have bypass surgery. Have cancer? Let's start eating healthy. This disease care is about reacting to the results that stem from poor health habits.

The proactive approach is deciding that you want to be healthy, figuring out what your definition of good health is, and then taking actions to get that result. Creating health is very different from reacting to health problems.

Creating is getting a result based on thoughts and actions that are in harmony with that result. Creating feels good.

Reacting to problems on the other hand, is like playing whack-a-mole. Something pops up you don't like, so you bop it on the head. The next thing pops up, and you bop it on the head. On and on it goes.

Bopping moles makes you feel like you are making progress and taking charge of your life, but this is part of the grand illusion to cover up the dark side of living reactively.

The inherent failing with the mole bopping game plan is that you never run out of moles. Even if by some miracle you did manage to get rid of every problem you have, now what? Now you have removed what you don't want, but you also don't have what you *do* want. You don't have a disease at the moment, but you don't have health either.

Making your list of problems and checking them off one at a time might make you feel like you are fixing your life, but the reality is that getting rid of problems leaves you with nothing but the absence of those problems.

Furthermore, the problem solving strategy has another built in defect that occurs because the motivation to fix a problem increases and decreases in direct correlation to the intensity of the problem.

Thus, when a problem feels intense in the beginning, your motivation to fix it is high, and you are inspired to take massive action. As the actions work, the problem shrinks, and you are proud of your willpower, discipline, and the results you see. You feel good.

That's because you don't yet see the hidden predicament you have created. As your actions are effective, the problem shrinks just like you wanted it to, but sadly your motivation to fix that problem shrinks right along with it. Ironically, you are now left in a position where the closer you get to eliminating the problem, the less motivation you have to do so.

This is how you are left with a life full of partially fixed problems and projects. It is also how you accidentally create up and down cycles in your life that fluctuate with the intensity of your problem du jour.

For example, if you chronically overspend and suddenly find yourself unable to make your payments, you feel the urgency to stop spending. The intensity of the problem is acute, so you psyche yourself up, have those talks with yourself, skip that new pair of shoes, and pass on dinners out with the friends. You do the required scrimping because you have to.

Slowly you catch up, one credit card paid off, then the next. Back on time with the car payment. That feels good doesn't it? The problem is gone. Unfortunately your motivation to be financially responsible is gone too. Next up... buying that new pair of shoes you "need" on your credit card, and the cycle starts all over again.

If you want to lose weight, it's easy to have that major motivation in the beginning when the problem feels intense. Thats how you end up in the gym at 5 am every morning. But what happens as the weight comes off?

Five pounds, ten pounds, twenty pounds gone. Everything is going according to plan, except that the closer you get to your goal, the less urgency you feel about being overweight, and the less motivation you have to keep on keeping on.

Suddenly it's not so important to hit the gym at 5 am. Suddenly eating that donut at work doesn't seem so bad. And suddenly you are right back where you were before, or worse.

But don't worry, you can always start the cycle all over again. And again. And again. Operating your life by reacting to problems is why you have the never ending up and down cycles. It's how your life becomes a pendulum swinging back and forth from one extreme to the other.

This is the hidden peril in reactively taking actions based on results, and it's why using your circumstances to motivate your actions is not the best way to improve your life.

The way off the merry-go-round is to stop reacting to circumstances, and start proactively taking actions based on thoughts about what you want. The goal then becomes to create what you want, not to eliminate your problems.

When your motivating force is getting what you want, your motivation increases rather than decreases as you get closer to your goal. That, as they say, makes all the difference.

Having a creative, proactive orientation does not mean your problems suddenly cease to exist. It does mean that they are no longer your focus, and they don't drive your worries and fears, or your strategy for creating a better life. You may still *think* you have problems, but they just don't matter much anymore. What you want becomes what matters instead.

When you proactively focus your thoughts on what you want, then your actions can organically flow from these thoughts and lead to the proper result.

When there is alignment and harmony between your thoughts, your actions, and the results you see, this is called congruence. When you have this congruence, the equation is simple, peaceful, and effective, and so is your life.

Let's say you love having a beautiful yard (thought), and enjoy trimming and mowing the grass (action), to get that nice lawn (result). In this case your beliefs, your actions, and the result you create are in harmony. This is congruence. It feels peaceful. You like it.

On the other hand, if you don't care how your yard looks, you may still mow and trim out of a sense of peer pressure from the neighbors, but now these actions are a source of distress rather than pleasure. Your thoughts, actions, and results are not in harmony. The incongruence feels wrong.

Congruency is desirable, but it only brings peace and happiness under the right circumstances. For example, let's say you have subconscious beliefs that you don't deserve abundance, that rich people are bad, that money is evil, or that someone else getting rich diminishes you somehow.

You likely then will take actions in your life based on those beliefs. You will surround yourself with people who lack abundance and consider successful people as lucky or bad. You may focus on scarcity, struggle financially, sabotage yourself with debt, and live a meager life. These are results created by actions that are driven by your thoughts about abundance.

In this case your software has created congruence, but not happiness. You have congruency with a poor result. This happens when hidden beliefs drive your behavior rather than true thoughts about what you want.

It is also possible that you might use your poverty as motivation to work hard at acquiring wealth. The problem is that the more wealth you acquire, the farther you get from what you believe, and from congruence. In this case, the results may be desirable, but they don't match your core beliefs.

This lack of congruence can lead to feelings of emptiness or unhappiness without knowing why, feeling that what you have is wrong or bad, that you don't deserve it, or that it might all be taken away from you.

Often the final result of these feelings is self-sabotage as your software does it's best to get you back to what you really believe. This is what comes from trying to force behavioral changes that are not in alignment with your belief system.

It's called swimming upstream.

On the other hand if you create new thoughts and beliefs about abundance, wealth, and money, then your actions can flow *naturally* and *organically* from those thoughts to create results you believe in. Now you can have abundance that feels good. Now you are swimming downstream.

The equation of life is a tool, a structure, a way of understanding how to get the life you want. Used properly it creates harmony, peacefulness, and happiness, but only if it is based on proactively created thoughts about what you want, rather than on junk that was programmed into your mind without your informed consent.

The equation gives you permission to decide whether your life is determined by thoughts or by results, by your preferred future or by your past, by design or by accident.

Which way you choose is like the difference between a rocket and a balloon. What happens when you blow up a balloon as far as it will go without bursting, and then let it go? You get a lot of noise, and a short, random, chaotic flight to the floor. The flight of the balloon feels messy, and unpredictable.

By contrast, a rocket flies towards a pre-programmed target in the most direct trajectory possible. A rocket feels like power, control, and predictability.

Question: Are you a rocket or a balloon?

Living a life reacting to results makes you a balloon. Creating a life based on what you want makes you the rocket.

You are the rocket when you understand the equation, decide what you want, and then work to create harmony between your thoughts, your actions, and your results.

You have the ability to think about how you think, to change how you think, and thus determine what your life becomes going forward.

You are a being made of thoughts. Everything you are, everything you have, and everything you do comes from your thoughts.

And who controls those thoughts?

Only you, my friend.

CHAPTER FIVE

The Happiness Cake

You want to be happy.

Happiness is when the pieces and parts of your life work together well enough to give you feelings of joy, fulfillment, peace, and serenity.

You want the right job, financial security, prestige, a nice home, and the material possessions you dream about. You would like good relationships, hobbies you love, spending your days doing things you enjoy, and living where you want to be. You want to be physically and mentally healthy, to feel good about who you are, and to be contributing to the world in a positive way.

These things and others are the conditions and circumstances of your life - the results you have created so far. If you are typical, you use these results like a barometer of happiness to show yourself and others how happy you are. It follows then that the search for happiness becomes a search for the right circumstances.

The conditions for happiness vary from person to person. One person's happy life is another's sad life. That's why there is no happiness blueprint to follow. No one can tell you how to be happy. You get to decide.

You need to bake your happiness cake using your own recipe.

When you are not happy, you search for reasons. The seductive tendency is to blame something outside of yourself - other people, upbringing, parents, spouse, children, boss, where you live, your schooling or lack of it, society, the government, the economy, your income level.

Giving credit to someone or something outside of yourself for your level of happiness seems so natural, so easy, so right. That's because it gives you reasons for things not being how you want them. It is a way for the ego to protect itself. Placing blame elsewhere means you don't have to look in the mirror and say, "I did this."

Blaming is easy and convenient. It's like an addictive drug that numbs you, takes away the pain, and feels good for awhile.

It also kills your life.

This is so because blaming gives the power to control your happiness away to whatever or whomever you are blaming - you can't be happy unless "they" let you be happy. That is why the blame game is a fool's game.

Fortunately, you can play a different game. The new game is about power. Not power over other things or other people, but rather over yourself and your destiny. It is the power that will leave you happy and fulfilled if you use it, and bring misery if you give it away.

This new super power can be yours, right now. It requires no physical effort on your part. The only requirement is that you make arguably the most important choice of your lifetime.

You have two options. One is to continue blaming external forces for your life, the other is to start taking RESPONSIBILITY for everything. All of it.

You can make that decision right now, can't you? Think carefully, because everything is at stake.

If you choose to continue with blame, excuses, denial, and rationalizing, then you will continue getting what you have gotten so far.

Choosing responsibility on the other hand, is the most powerful choice you can make because it instantly frees you from all of the oppressive forces you thought were controlling you all this time. Instantly. Free.

This happens because if *you* created the life you *now* have, that means you have the power to create the life you *will* have. If you created this, then you can create that. If you took actions that got you where you are now, you can take different actions to get somewhere else.

Alternatively, if you choose to believe that someone or something else is responsible for your life, then you are powerless to do anything about it. You are a victim subject to the whims of other people and your past.

Granted, many of your past choices and actions have been dictated or influenced by the hidden software, and you may feel the need to place blame there. Don't. Accepting responsibility means accepting it for everything, including things you didn't know about. Responsibility is absolute. You either blame, or be responsible - but not both. Your past does not absolve you from taking responsibility for your future.

A powerful, beautiful truth in the universe is that you are the creative force behind your own life. This becomes true for you when you think it's true, and it becomes possible when you choose responsibility over blame.

Like everything else, responsibility is a thought. When you believe in responsibility, you will take different actions than when you don't, and you will accordingly receive different results.

Becoming responsible is not a penance, nor should it need to feel bad. If you are unhappy with your life now, then realize that the circumstances you created so far are the ones you needed to create. You could not have gotten to where you are, nor can you get to where you are going, without coming the way you came.

Your current circumstances and problems do not define who you are, or determine where you can go. They are not your enemies, but rather friends that will help you see how your choices have led you to where you are. They are the key to discovering the beliefs and thought processes driving your life, and exposing how aligned or misaligned you are with the natural forces.

Each result you see around you contains a lesson about how you got it, and finding that lesson is how you use those results to stop your past from determining your future.

You get to decide if your life will be spent complaining about the circumstances you have, or creating the ones you want. Will results control you, or will you control them?

Will your level of happiness be dictated to you, or determined by you?

It's your life. Bake your own happiness cake, using your own recipe.

Then take responsibility for how it tastes.

CHAPTER SIX

A Perfectly Possible Day

How you spend your days is how you spend your life.

When I was a little boy, I loved spending my days sleeping in as long as possible. Getting up in the morning was always a chore, and most times I would lay in bed partially awake, struggling through the grogginess and thinking about the day ahead... how cold the floor would feel on my feet, getting ready for school, the bus ride. Was my homework finished? Would I have to talk in class? Would kids tease me? Slowly the stress and tension would build and finally snap me to full awake, feeling the dread. Why can't I just stay here, safe in my nice warm bed?

But on some mornings, I would be drifting in and out of sleep when a sound would slowly begin to penetrate the fogginess in my head. What's that noise? Could it be? YES! It's the faint sound of bacon frying in the kitchen.

Trying to believe my ears, I would breathe in deeply to catch the delicious bacon smell drifting down the hall and into my bedroom. And that's when it would hit me. Holy cow… it's Saturday!

There's no school, there's no homework, there's no stress today. There is just a wonderful day full of boundless opportunities, fun, excitement, playing, happiness.

I would bound out of bed with the enthusiasm that even our dog couldn't match in the morning. Down the hall I went, and sure enough, there's mom in her fluffy white bathrobe, carefully tending the bacon on the stove. She turns and smiles love at me.

Sunlight is streaming through the big window, showing off the dust particles floating in the air, and making the whole room feel warm and bright and cheery. I look around and take a deep breath. It's true. Everything is alright. It's going to be a great day. It's Saturday!

As the years went by, I mostly forgot about the Saturday morning feeling as it faded to a distant, almost unreal memory - a treat reserved only for children, I supposed.

Every once in awhile though, it would come back to me with feelings of fondness and sadness, and I would wonder why life wasn't meant to feel that way every day, and why a lifetime couldn't be filled mostly with Saturday morning days.

Then the one day when it happened, I didn't want to ignore the possibility anymore, so I thought about what it would take for just one day to feel like that again. What would a perfect day in my life be like? What would I do, how would I feel, who would I be with, and where would I be on that one perfect day?

I didn't filter or restrain my thinking. I didn't worry about what was possible or not. I didn't care anymore what other people might think about my day. I just wanted to FEEL what one perfect day would be like... and I wondered whether it was reasonable to expect to pull off a perfect day here and there.

I decided that it was.

That got me to thinking more... if I could have a perfect day once in awhile, why couldn't I put together a perfect day, say once a week? Maybe even twice a week? This inevitably led to the elephant in the room question - why can't I have a perfect day, every day?

Why can't every day feel like Saturday morning?

Of course we all know that can't happen, right? And we know this because... umm... well... because that's just the way it is?

But what if, just for a moment, we could ignore our limiting beliefs about what is possible? What if we could put all of our self-imposed restraints aside for just a little while, and write a simple story about perfect days like it's perfectly possible.

So that's what I did. I wrote a story about my perfectly possible days... in sparkling detail. How much cash do I have in the bank? What is my monthly income? Am I working, and if so, doing what? What do I do on my perfect day? Who do I surround myself with? What is my home like? Where do I live? What is my spouse like? What hobbies do I have? What is my contribution towards making the world better? What do I eat? How much do I exercise? How much do I sleep? What does my daily schedule look like? How do I feel each day?

After I wrote my story, I felt relief that it was out in the open. I felt good, because Saturday morning days somehow seemed possible again. I felt happy, as if a long lost friend had finally come home to breathe peace and possibility into my soul again.

Writing a story about perfect days changed my life.

You can write a story about perfect days too, can't you?

The hard part is letting go of self-imposed limitations. The trap is censoring your thoughts and beliefs about what is possible. Don't do that. Just for a little while, just this once, give yourself a break. Cut you some slack. Give yourself permission to dream big. It's just a story after all, so make it a good one. Make it yours and no one else's.

It's the most important thing in your life right now.

It's your clear and compelling dream.

CHAPTER SEVEN

Mountain Climbing

You and I are going on a trip through the mountains.

It will be imaginary and real, and the most important trip of your lifetime. But before we set off, imagine for a moment that you are standing alone on top of a mountain. Let's call it REALITY MOUNTAIN.

Now, gaze down across the hazy valley stretching out far and away below you. Off in the distance see the majestic mountain towering above all others, shining like a beacon with the sun glimmering off its peak. You see it out there, don't you? This is DREAM MOUNTAIN.

Reality mountain represents your life as it is right now - inside and out. It is the sum of everything you are and everything you have.

Dream mountain represents your ideal life, filled with your perfectly possible days.

Reality mountain is where you are, and dream mountain is where you want to go. Between the two lies the trip called life.

The journey to dream mountain is why you are here - it is your destiny. The trip is beautiful in its own perfect way, yet fraught with all the difficulties we bring upon ourselves by virtue of being human.

You cannot walk a simple straight line to dream mountain. You need to encounter all of the terrain along the way. You may have to drag yourself across a desert, slog through some swamp, hike up some hills, fight your way through the brambles, and wade through some creeks. You could get caught in a wild river that takes you miles downstream. Here and there you will trip and fall flat on your face. There will be blood.

None of that matters.

If there is a quicksand pit try not to walk into it, but if you do, call out and help will come for you. On the path to dream mountain, help always comes when you need it.

Is it going to be an easy trip? Maybe. Is it going to be hard? Maybe. Easy means your dream is pulling hard at you. Hard means you have more work to do to be worthy of your dream. Easy or hard doesn't matter either.

What matters is that you keep your eyes focussed on dream mountain as you move relentlessly and ruthlessly towards it, and that you deal with whatever shows up in front of you when it is time for you to do so.

If you get lost in the swamp, look for dream mountain peeking over the treetops and go that way. When the wild river sweeps you miles downstream, crawl up on the far shore, shake yourself off, look to see where dream mountain is now, and take off towards it again. When the surrounding foothills block your view, hike up the nearest one until you can see dream mountain again.

No matter what is in front of you, no matter where you are, no matter what you need to go through, dream mountain is always there, standing ready to guide you.

But you have to move.

You can stare over at dream mountain and ponder its beauty endlessly. You can sit on your perch and think about dream mountain all day. You can wish and hope to be there, pray and meditate about it, or talk to your friends about your intent until you're blue in the face. You can study the terrain below with binoculars forever as you fill notebooks with your plans and schemes and routes.

None of that will get you anywhere. Until you take a step towards dream mountain, nothing is ever going to happen. Not ever.

Here is your itinerary: Know where you are now, have a clear and compelling dream, get moving. Take a step, adjust. Take a step, adjust. Take a step, adjust. Put one foot in front of the other and move steadily and relentlessly towards the dream until you are there. That's it.

What do we do instead? We make up lists of things to do and problems to solve before we go. We plan, stall, make excuses, and rationalize. We sit on our mountain afraid. We look at all the "normal" people around us living their own lives of quiet desperation, and convince ourselves it's really not so bad on reality mountain after all.

Instead of doing that, take a step. It's for you, and for the world that will be without your special contribution if you don't. Do not live a life that doesn't matter as much as it could because you're a big fat chicken.

If you *are* afraid, that's fine, but take a step anyway. You need not fear the consequences of your step because when your clear and compelling dream is guiding you, all actions you take inherently work to your benefit.

Some actions bring you closer to your dream, and these build momentum, confidence, and speed. They show you what works for you.

Some actions move you farther from your dream, but this is not something to fear or feel bad about. Actions that push you farther from your dream increase the motivational energy available to you. Correcting what doesn't work grows you as a person and teaches you new lessons. Overcoming obstacles builds strength, confidence, pride, and self esteem. Struggling through the terrain evolves you into a better human.

The hardships make it so you deserve your dream when you get there, and when you deserve your dream, it cannot be taken from you.

When your eyes are firmly fixed on dream mountain, you inherently cannot make a mistake regardless of what actions you take - but you have to move.

You must reach for your dream, and when you do, your dream will reach for you. What you are looking for is looking for you. But if you don't move, if you don't take action, then you are just another person with a dream that will never happen.

Yes, stuff will come up as you move. Stuff that you need to figure out, deal with, and take actions on. Stuff that bothers you, maybe even hurts you. But don't worry about that.

When you are going from where you are to where you want to be, you have to do the stuff in between. It can be no other way. Stuff is neither good nor bad. It's not a problem, a barrier, or a reason to not do something. Stuff is just stuff.

The dream compels you do to do more, have more, be more. It grows you. The bigger your dream and the farther it is from your current reality, the more stuff you will have to go through, and the more you will have to grow to achieve it. It doesn't matter. That's how it works. That's how it's supposed to work.

That is why big dreams are better.

You need clarity about reality mountain and clarity about dream mountain. Once those are cemented in your mind, the rest is just stuff between the two.

In between your reality and your dream stand the dream killers. You already know them intimately - fear, doubt, excuses, rationalization, denial, and the people who want you as you are, who doubt you, who are trapped by their own mental images about their own limitations.

These dream killers have only the power you give them. They can be gone like gremlins in the blink of an eye, in the nanosecond it takes you to change a thought.

Change comes as fast as you can change your mind about what you believe.

This discrepancy between where you are now and where you want to be, between what you have and what you want, can be an immense source of frustration. You want to win the lottery to make that uncomfortable discrepancy go away, because you think this distance is your enemy. It isn't.

This distance is what creates the energy that will pull you to your dream. The farther your dream is from your reality, the more energy there is to help you. The available energy depends on two factors.

The first is how clear and compelling your dream is. How badly do you want it? How much do you love it? Is it something you really want, or is it something you've talked yourself into wanting, or something your parents want for you, or something you think you're *supposed* to want?

The second factor is how accurately you see your current reality. You need to know where you are, who you are, and what you want - clearly. This is what creates the force that will move you.

The force is strongest when you keep a clear, accurate picture of your reality and of your dream in your mind at the same time, and do not waver from either - no matter the discomfort you may feel.

When you can do this, the magic in the universe will pull you towards your dream, and the stuff, the how, will happen - if you let it.

Such is the power of dreams.

If your life feels wrong in some way, if you are struggling, floundering, hurt, or confused, it's because you don't see your clear and compelling dream, you are not moving towards it, or both.

You need to know where you are. You need to know where you are going. You need to take a step.

That is all.

CHAPTER EIGHT

Reality Mountain

You can't get where you are going until you know where you are.

If you were blindfolded and placed in the middle of a four way intersection somewhere far away, given a map and a car, and told to drive to Chicago, could you do it?

Oh sure, you could easily find Chicago on the map, but until you know where *you* are on the map relative to Chicago, you can't know whether to head north, south, east or west. You don't know the correct direction until you first know where you are.

Where you are is called reality, and this is always the starting point because no matter where you want to go, you must begin from where you are.

Reality has an inner component and an outer component. The outer reality is everything you see when you look around - your material possessions, your geographic location, your job, income, savings, house, family, etc.

The inner reality includes your mental state, level of happiness, goals, character, personality, attitudes, values, emotions, thoughts, and beliefs. The inner reality is about who you are, and how you perceive and interact with the world around you.

The inner reality determines the outer reality, and thus is far and away the more important of the two, but it is the outer that we tend to focus on and fret about. We want the outer things to fix the inner things, when in fact the opposite is required.

Seeing the outer reality is simple - just look around. On the other hand, gaining a clear, undistorted, honest picture of the inner reality is tricky... and critically important.

When you don't clearly see your reality, you move without knowing whether it's the right direction. You make decisions and take actions based on false information and perceptions. You build a house of cards life on a shaky foundation that keeps moving and shifting.

Seeing reality clearly is an art, a learned skill, and a process that requires the honesty and courage to cut through all the nonsense you tell yourself and others all the time.

This matters because you were born a pure soul with a purpose, and that pure soul is still in there. But a lifetime of living, getting beat up, making mistakes, and absorbing poor knowledge, has added layers and layers of crap upon your soul.

That lifetime has also given you software that created a security blanket to surround and protect your ego from the discomfort of confronting reality head on. It gave you the ability to mentally distort reality, and special tools to use for that purpose. The software creates a cloud of confusion about where you are, who you are, and what you really want.

When reality mountain is covered by that cloud, you can't see dream mountain. You can't see anything. You wander aimlessly in circles, up and down, this way and that, never actually getting anywhere.

The cloud is lifted by gaining a clear understanding of your reality, and this is a critical undertaking for many reasons...

If you don't know how you want your life to be, how will you avoid deathbed regrets?

If you aren't aware of the software programs how are you going to fix them? How are you going to get the bugs and viruses out?

If you don't understand the equation of life and how thoughts cause the actions that create results, how are you going to stop the never ending up and down cycles in your life?

If you don't know what would give you congruence, how can you have it?

If you can't find your secret happiness recipe, how can you bake the happiness cake?

If you don't decide what one perfectly possible day would be like, how can you create a lifetime filled with them?

If you don't know why you do what you do, how will you stop doing things that damage you and yours?

If you don't know where you are, how can you possibly get where you want to be?

If you don't know what you stand for, what you value, what you want, and who you are, then you are destined to spend your life walking circles in a murky haze, reacting to stimuli, getting your buttons pushed, and living someone else's agenda.

Once clarity lifts the cloud off reality mountain, then you can see dream mountain and feel the distance between the two. This is when the energy that pulls you toward your dream is generated.

Clarity was easy for you as a child, but then life happened. Children speak their reality clearly - "mom says you don't have any money," or "your house smells funny." They speak truths that adults are uncomfortable with, and so we quickly and efficiently train them not to do that. That is what happened to you, and that is where it all started breaking bad.

We were all trained from childhood to distort reality, and as adults we do it well for many reasons. We do it to avoid discomfort, to cover mistakes or incompetence, to protect our fragile ego, and to hide our perceived shortcomings.

We do it because our damaged self esteem tells us we are not good enough the way we are, and that others are more successful or better somehow. We do it because we care too much about how others see us, and fear their rejection, judgement, or ridicule. We do it because we are human.

Some of the common reality distortion tools we use are denial, blame, rationalization, and excuses. They can sound like this:

Distortion: I don't drink much alcohol.

Reality: The recycle bin is full of empty beer cans.

Distortion: I only buy what I need.

Reality: Your credit cards are maxed out.

Distortion: I'm overweight but I eat healthy.

Reality: Your desk drawer is full of chips and candy.

Distortion: I need a new vehicle because _____.

Reality: You want a new vehicle.

Distortion: I'm late for work because traffic is bad.

Reality: You don't leave for work early enough.

Distortion: I don't have time to exercise.

Reality: You don't have control over your time.

Distortion: It's not my fault I cheated on my spouse.

Reality: It is your fault.

Distortion: I hate my job, but I'm stuck with it.

Reality: You can do something else.

Reality distortions are lies you tell yourself. They may not seem like lies to you, but they are. The more you lie to yourself, the better you become at it, the more you believe the lies, and the less you are able to see them.

These distortions and others like them are difficult to self recognize because they are a part of you. They make sense to you. You've made them legitimate - so much so that you probably even find it irritating to be challenged about them. They are woven into the fabric of your life to the point that you can't see them.

But you can see them in other people, can't you? You see theirs, just as they see yours. Less evolved people may point them out to you in harsh ways, creating conflict and hurt feelings. More evolved people may simply accept and understand. Those who love you enough are the ones who will show you your distortions with the intent of helping you... if you let them.

Learning to see your own distortions is a fine art. As you struggle for clarity and learn to speak the truth to yourself, your distortions will begin to reveal themselves. One by one they will bark at you. You can acknowledge them, thank them for barking, and then make them go away.

A life based on too many distortions is characterized by confusion, stress, a lack of honesty with self and others, and inability to move forward. Distortions create an inner reality that is a jumbled up mess. If you want calmness, peace, and serenity, you have to make the mess go away, and the way you do that is through honesty and clarity.

The first step is changing your mind about reality. Reality is not your enemy, or the bad guy, or something to fear or hide from. Reality is truth, and thus inherently cannot be bad.

If you feel bad about your current situation, then realize that poor circumstances do not define who you are. They are simply an indicator of the choices you have made so far, based on your software programming.

The key is understanding that accepting responsibility for the circumstances you have now is what gives you the power to create new ones. If you created the life you have, you can create the life you will have.

If you won't accept responsibility, then your circumstances are just something else to bitch about. If you do accept responsibility, your circumstances become a useful tool in your battle for inner truth.

If you have no money, what thoughts and beliefs created that? The lack of abundance is a symptom begging you to find the beliefs that caused it. If your relationships end in failure, you are not healthy, you are estranged from your parents or siblings, you cheat or lie, you are not living a big enough life, or if you are not doing what you want to be doing, then realize that these are outer circumstances reflecting inner reality. Somewhere there are thoughts that need repairing.

The repair process begins by realizing that at the core you are a good person with the right to be who you are. Your soul is pure.

You will discover the purity once you strip away all the layers of clutter and junk that were programmed into you without your consent. You will see it when you strip yourself naked and stand unblinking in the bright lights of reality, knowing that you have nothing to be ashamed of, and nothing to fear.

When you can whittle yourself down to your purest form and shed all the miscellaneous layers that have been piled on your soul over the years, then you have a good, honest place to move forward from.

You can start this process right now. Find a quiet place where you can sit and think. Close your eyes and quiet your mind. Imagine that nothing matters anymore. Let your worries, fears, and responsibilities drift away. Your current circumstances don't matter. Your past doesn't matter. It doesn't matter at all what other people think about you. All that matters is you. Strip your mind clean of all judgement and thoughts about what is possible or not. Think about perfectly possible days and who you are in your perfect life. There are no limits or boundaries. Nothing matters. Let the layers slip away quietly, until all you feel is you.

Now say who you are.

"I am_____," (finish the sentence). If your dream is to be a writer then say it. I am a writer. Or I am a painter. I am a loving wife. I am happy. I am educated. I am a millionaire. I am a world traveler. I am a famous dog trainer. I am a master gardener.

Say it like you mean it. Say it as if it were already so. Keep finishing the sentence over and over until you have no more answers. Talk as if the world were perfect, and you were perfect. Don't talk about who you appear to be now, talk about who you are.

Next, write across the top of a sheet of paper in big, bold letters, **THIS IS WHO I AM**, and then write down all of your answers. There are no right or wrong answers. All that matters is honesty and purity. The soul knows. Listen to it.

Do the exercise again every day or every other day, letting your answers evolve and change as they feel like it. Right before bed is best so that your subconscious mind can stew all night about who you really are. Look at your list again in the morning, so that it influences the choices you make that day.

While writing and thinking about your list, visualize how you will feel when you are living according to who you are, and doing what you are supposed to be doing. Dream about a life filled with perfect days. Notice the peace and relief that comes when you realize that it's OK to be who you are, and your soul finally feels understood.

This battle for clarity is about honesty. It is about cutting through all the bullshit and lies we all like to tell ourselves. When you can accept truth as it is, when you can stop caring what others might think, when you can stop lying to yourself, then you are free.

The more you work at seeing it, the clearer your reality becomes. The clearer reality becomes, the more peaceful you feel, and the better your life goes.

Life is different once you have clarity and acceptance about your reality. A weight lifts off of you when you stop punishing yourself for who you are and where you are, and realize that honesty about reality is not bad.

Nothing bad comes from telling yourself the truth. If you drink too much, instead of making excuses about it, just admit it and move on. If you are fat because you eat too much and don't exercise, just say that. On the way to being late for work again, listen to the excuses you are telling yourself and just stop already.

When the voice in your head tells you all the reasons and excuses about why you can't have the life you want - stop. Think. Understand, that this is reality being distorted by your software.

You are free to continue on using denial, blame, justifications, and excuses as reasons to stay where you are. You can choose to be afraid of honesty, or not. You get to decide whether reality is your enemy or your friend - it is whatever you think it is. One way is upstream, the other down. Your choice.

When the dust settles and you have acceptance and peace about who you are, then you are free to step towards your better life, and to build new layers upon your pure soul by design, rather than by accident.

Once you understand who you are, then you can start being who you are.

Be clear.

Be honest.

Be free.

CHAPTER NINE

Dream Mountain

Your dream is why you are here.

You don't need to invent your dream. It's already inside you, waiting patiently for you to find it and let it out. But sometimes it's hard to see it in there, isn't it.

Maybe you don't know what you want. Or perhaps you are so caught up in day to day living that there doesn't seem to be time for your dream right now. No worries though, you'll get to it later... right?

Possibly you work harder at keeping the dream bottled up inside than it would be to just let it out. That's because of all the crap that has been beaten into your head since you were born about what is possible, about what you deserve, your intelligence, your aptitude, your worth, money, hard work, greed.

To get to your dream, you've got to throw all of that out. You've got to overcome all the junk your parents told you. You need to deal with subconscious feelings of not being good enough. You must convince your heart and your mind that you deserve what you want, and that it's OK to write your story about perfectly possible days.

You also need to become aware of how the software created by your past influences your dream, and your future.

For example, let's say you decide to turn up your financial thermostat by declaring that your dream is to have a million dollars in the bank. Since your dream speaks for your soul, you know this is certainly a worthy ambition.

But what happens if you set that goal, while at the same time your subconscious mind believes that money is the root of all evil, that you should feel guilty about having it, that it's not fair to other people, that you don't deserve it, that it is wrong, selfish, greedy, or simply not possible?

In such a case, your dream helped you create a thought about what you want, but the new thought doesn't jibe with your old software. Now you have a conflict between your belief system and your dream - your programming is arguing with your soul.

If you are not aware of the software, you don't even know the argument is going on. All you know is that you are stressed, confused, and don't understand why you can't get your life coherently moving in the right direction.

Awareness is critical because if these beliefs are not exposed, an entire lifetime might be spent unaware that it was controlled all the while by hidden software.

Your dream is what brings this awareness. It is the force that will finally confront your software and drive hidden thoughts, beliefs, and conflicts into the open where you can see them.

Clarifying and committing to your dream is how you turn up your internal thermostat, and thus force the epic showdown between what you say you want and what you believe. This is when your dream says it is OK for you to have what you want, be who you are, and do what you love - but your programming says its not.

And yes, in a showdown, things can get ugly. You might not like it. You might be afraid, or angry, or confused. You could have doubts about yourself and your dream. You may think about turning the thermostat back down or even switching sides.

But you shouldn't, because your dream is right.

Your programming is largely an accident. Your dream is not. Your dream will win, if you stand tall, don't flinch, be brave, and focus on what you want.

At some point on the path to dream mountain, you will no doubt come to this showdown fork in the trail. Choosing to side with your old software is the way back to reality mountain. Choosing to side with your dream continues you on your way to dream mountain.

When you are standing at the fork, remember that reality mountain was largely created for you by the software. In many ways, it's an accident, and an illusion posing as who you are.

Your dream on the other hand, comes from your soul. It is the essence of who you are, and it gives you the power to create your preferred future. You claim this future by clarifying your dream, and having the courage and drive to step boldly towards it.

The dream is is inside you, and it is what you want, even if you don't know it yet, or won't admit it, or don't think it's possible. And it's got to come out if you are to have the life you are meant to live.

If your dream has been hiding inside, it's time to invite it out to play in the sunshine. Start by finding a pen and paper and a peaceful place where you can be calm and comfortable. Take a moment to clear your head and relax. Be open to letting your thoughts flow freely and without reservation. Feel some excitement begin to simmer inside you around the possibilities for your future.

When you are ready, write in big letters across the top of the paper, THIS IS WHAT I WANT. Then write down everything you want. Everything. A big long list. Write fast and freely, don't think too much, and don't hold anything back.

This is your dream list.

The goal is to write what you want. Nothing more. Nothing less. No judgements. No distortions. No limits. No bullshit. Write about how you want to feel, who you want to be, what you want to have, and how you want to spend your days. Write honestly about everything you have ever wanted, and everything you will ever want.

Keep writing until nothing more comes to mind, but under no circumstances should you stop before you have at least twenty things on your list.

Don't make the mistake of thinking that your dream list doesn't need to be written. Vague notions in your head won't cut it. Telling yourself that you know what you want doesn't work. Until it is written, it isn't real. If you cannot make yourself sit down and write a list of at least twenty things you want, then you need to go sit in a corner somewhere until you figure out why that is.

Give yourself permission to want whatever you want. If you want something, don't try to talk yourself out of it, don't judge it, don't think about it at all - just write it down. You can't make yourself not want something you want anyway, you can only deceive yourself about it. Deceiving yourself about it is distorting your reality. Stop doing that.

What you think is possible, or what your parents or friends think, or what you would have to do to get what you want, are irrelevant concepts here. None of that changes the reality about what you want.

Do not limit your list to what you think is possible. Things are only impossible until they're not, and you can't know what is possible or not possible for you until you've tried.

Granted, it could be that what you want really isn't possible. If you are blind, you want to see. If you are in a wheelchair, you want to walk. Maybe you want to fly by flapping your arms. These wants may not be possible, but that doesn't change the reality that you want them.

Don't lie to yourself. Don't deny. Yes it's true that there will be things on your list that you may never have, and it is healthy and wise to accept that premise. Still, the list must be honest. If you want it, write it down.

Do not list compromises. If your dream is to be a master chef, don't write about being a fry cook because you think you can't afford school right now. That is limiting your dream to what you think is possible and reasonable. Your soul does not want to invest in compromise.

Do not write down what you don't want... I don't want to be poor, I don't want to be sick, I don't want to be in debt. These thoughts put your focus on what you don't want rather than on what you do want, and what you focus on is what you get more of. Keep your focus on what you want.

Don't write about getting rid of problems either. This is just another way of focussing on what you don't want. Getting rid of problems leaves you with nothing but the absence of problems.

Don't think about *how* you might get something you want, because this limits your thinking to what you already know. Getting what you want may require learning things you don't know yet, and doing things you haven't done before. Don't worry about the how, now. Clarify what you want first, and how comes later.

Also do not focus on how another person should be or act, because you have no control over other people. When it comes to others, write only about the nature and quality of the relationships you want with them.

In other words, don't say, "I want my son to go to college." Say instead, "I want to be a good parent and help my son make good decisions." Don't say, "I want my spouse to stop being a jerk." Say instead, "I want a loving relationship with my spouse."

Finally, don't try to explain or justify what you want or why you want it - not to yourself, and not to anyone else. If you have a reason for wanting what you want, that's great, but you don't need one. You can think about why later, but not now.

There is no requirement that you understand why the things on your dream list are there, or why they are important. Perhaps what you want is bubbling up from a deep place in the universe that you can't know about or understand. Maybe there is a master plan that you aren't privy to. Possibly you need to evolve to where it all makes sense.

For now, simply be honest about what you want, trust that things are how they should be, know that there is nothing wrong with what you want, and understand that you are part of a perfect system.

There is a certain peace that comes once you realize that you are free to want whatever you want, without reasons, reservations, or limits. It happens when you stop with the endless barrage of crap, conflict, and confusion revolving around what you want, and just let it all be OK, for no reason.

As you create your list, try to feel for any beliefs that cause tension or conflict. This is your dream bringing awareness about your software. Listen for the limiting thoughts that pop into your head - thoughts that sound like this:

I could never do that.

That's impossible.

My parents would kill me if I did that.

My friends would hate me.

I can't just pack up and move.

I'm too old.

I'm too young.

I shouldn't want that.

That's not realistic.

I can't do that, because first I would have to _____.

I can't do that because I never went to college.

I have to put my children or spouse first.

I'm not smart enough.

I'm not good at _____.

I've got too many other responsibilities right now.

I don't have time.

I don't have the money.

My spouse won't support me.

These are the thoughts that come out of hiding when your dream forces them to. They are the gremlins in your head that keep you from what you want. These thoughts and others like them have influenced where you are today and where you will be ten years from now. Shine the bright light of reality on them, and they will dry up and wither away.

Your dream list may be fuzzy at first. You may not feel comfortable writing it. That's normal. That's why you should rewrite it every day.

The list is coming from deep within you, and it must fight its way through all the stuff inside you to get to the surface in pure form. That is why you can't force your list, anymore than you can force a rose to bloom faster.

As you write it over and over, simply let it mature, grow, and evolve. Over time, the cream will rise to the top and the list will gel. Let it be what it wants to be.

Your dream list is powerful because as it works its way to the surface, it helps you understand yourself and forces you to deal with your issues. It pushes you to search for truth, and confront deep seated beliefs. It forces your distortions out of the dark corners they hide in, and makes them bark at you so you can see them.

The mechanical, intellectual, and emotional act of writing THIS IS WHAT I WANT on top of a sheet of paper every day, and then listing your wants, is a powerful and almost effortless way to reprogram your subconscious mind.

This is how you start to rewrite the software running your life, and begin peeling the layers of crap off your pure soul. This is what brings you clarity, focus, and peace. Your dream list helps you with all of this, as it fights its way through the layers to take its rightful place at the forefront of everything you do.

If you will do your list diligently, even for a little while, you will be shocked at how many items on your dream list come to fruition within a year, seemingly without effort or conscious action.

This is not magic. It happens because processing your list leads your subconscious mind down a different path. Changing your thinking leads to different actions, and thus different results.

Over time, your true wants will rise to the top and separate themselves from those that don't belong because they are someone else's wants for you, because they are things you thought you were *supposed* to want, or because it turns out you never really wanted them in the first place.

You may also come to find things on your list that don't matter to you anymore, or are not really an end result you want, but rather only a step on the way to something else. Let these dissolve away peacefully.

As your list evolves and settles, it becomes appropriate to start asking why. Is it really the million dollars you want, or is it what you think the money will get you? Is it the big house you want, or is it the prestige that comes with it? If it's prestige you want, why?

You don't need a reason to want something, but asking the why questions for each item on your list brings clarity and helps you drill down to your authentic dream list.

One of the quicksand traps you may fall into on your path is thinking that your dream should be subordinated to the needs of your loved ones, that your dream list is selfish, or that it conflicts with what your spouse, children, friends, or others want.

This is a flawed mindset because it is based on an either/or scenario that doesn't exist. It assumes that either you get what you want, or they get what they want. But your dream isn't about either/or, it's about *and*. You get what you want, *and* they get what they want. That's how dreams work.

If you have ever flown on a commercial plane, then you know that in an emergency the oxygen masks drop down. In such a case, your inclination would be to help your loved ones get their mask on before tending to yours. But every stewardess before every flight tells you that is exactly the wrong thing to do. Why? Because if you pass out you won't be able to help them at all. You've got to put your own mask on first, and then help the others.

You are a good person and you want to help those you love. You don't mind sacrificing or putting their needs first. You probably would do anything for them. But if you really love them, put your own oxygen mask on first.

Denying what you want for the sake of others is unnecessary, and unfair to you and them. Many times it is simply a cop out. Do not insult your people by using them as an excuse to not follow your dream.

The high moral duty of every individual is to be happy. Being stifled, stressed, resentful, or unhappy is not good for you or anyone else on the planet.

Getting what you want improves your life, brings you happiness, improves you as a person, and allows you to be a better person for those around you. Getting what you want allows others to get what they want.

Your dream matters. It matters more than anything else. It goes to the core of your being. It is why you are here, and nothing should stand in the way of it, especially not the people you love.

If you really want to help those you love the most, then be an example, not a martyr.

When you operate from a place of clarity and pure intention, your dream can never be to the detriment of another. While short term sacrifices may be required, your dream always helps and never hurts others. Dreams are good, always.

There need be no guilt associated with what you want or dream about. Just like everyone else, you have the right to partake in all of the abundance the world has to offer.

It is not selfish or improper to desire material things, a better life, or anything else you want. Abundance is the desired, natural, healthy state of being.

Living a life of scarcity does no good for you, your loved ones, or the rest of the world. Scarcity is not a badge of honor, it is a sign that you need better software.

There are no limits on abundance, which is why your level of abundance does not detract from someone else's. You are free to pursue any level of abundance you like without fear of harm to others.

In the same way, the abundance of others does not detract from yours. If you believe it does, then your programming is leading you to false assumptions about wealth.

Someone else's richness has zero affect on your ability to live an abundant life and have what you want. Rich people are rich for a reason. It's because they have rich people software, and you can have it too if you want it.

Besides, is it really other people that are keeping you from your dream, or is it you keeping you from your dream? Do you not have your dream because it's not possible, or because you think it's not possible? Is it the reality of the world holding you back, or is it you holding you back?

Is your your dream kept bottled up inside because of fear, doubt, low self-esteem, feelings that you are not worthy? Because of some bullshit thoughts someone planted in your head when you were a kid? Because something you did or didn't do in the past didn't work out? Are these the thoughts that will keep you from your dream, from your reason for being, from your destiny? Is that the story you want to write? Why?

You don't need to live like a sheep, blindly following the masses, and living out your life doing what you are "supposed" to be doing based on what other people think.

You don't need to live a life based on programming that you didn't write, or be a bit player in someone else's story. Write your own.

When your deep mind aligns with your dream, when you take away your self imposed limitations, when you realize that your dream is supposed to happen, when you understand that your dream helps those around you, when you clear the roadblocks in your head, then your dream will come for you - peacefully, elegantly, and powerfully.

I knew I wanted to be a writer since I was a child. It was always something I was going to do... someday. You know, once I got the more "important" things out of the way.

I vividly remember the day that I decided that the common sense thing for me to do was first get a career to make money, and then get to my writing later. It is a choice that has haunted me since the day I made it.

One decade passed, and then many more. It makes me sick. I could have spent another decade, or the rest of my life wanting to write a book but never doing it. And on my last day I would have had to look in the mirror and ask the dreaded question - WHY NOT? Because I was worried no one would like it? Because someone might think it's stupid? Because I was afraid or embarrassed to express my thoughts to others?

I think those excuses would sound pretty feeble on my deathbed.

How are your excuses going to sound on your deathbed?

Write your dream list.

CHAPTER TEN

The Trip

Would you like to create a masterpiece?

A long time ago I needed new carpeting, and my search for a good deal brought me to a small store. A middle aged man with grey hair greeted me with a hardy handshake as he explained that he was the owner, and would be happy to show me around. He was a friendly chap, and we made small talk as he meandered me through his store, all the while extolling the virtues of this carpet and that.

At one point, his hand absentmindedly dropped to caress a roll of carpet hanging from the wall and he said almost reverently, "This is a very nice carpet...very nice."

He seemed to drift away, as if thinking about something that happened long ago, and then he spoke again in a slow, soft voice... "I love carpet. I don't know why, I just do. Always have. I love how it feels, the smell, all the colors and patterns. And I get to help people find just the right carpet that makes their house feel like their home. A nice carpet makes for a nice home..."

His voice trailed off as he came back to present, his face embarrassed like he had just said something foolish. I stood silently staring, because in that instant I had glimpsed the soul of a man doing what he is supposed to be doing.

It wasn't the greatest or the biggest store. I don't know how well it was managed, or if it was even profitable for him. I only know he was a man living what he loved, and for a brief moment I felt what that was like. I never forgot.

To me, carpet is just something I pay for to put on my floor. For many people who own or work in carpet stores, it's just something they sell to make money. You can spot people like that everywhere, in all businesses, all the time. And that is the difference between them, and this man doing his passion and living on purpose.

You've seen passion and purpose too. It's in the eyes of the woodworker as he painstakingly cuts and forms the perfect wood joint. It's the graphic designer working late into the night, unaware of time gone by. It's the guitar player practicing the same riff over and over until it's perfect, just because he wants to. It's the gardener carefully tending to her perfectly manicured flower garden. It's in the person who practices her craft in her dreams.

You have something that makes you feel on purpose too - a craft, a profession, a hobby, a sport, a charity, a nice lawn, a healthy family, a beautiful home, a flower garden, writing, painting, photography, music. These are things you enjoy, and would love to fill your perfect days with.

If you golf well, you created that skill. If you have a nice home or a nice family, you created that. You created your skills, your health, your lifestyle, your business, and your hobbies. These creations are the result of your previous thoughts and actions.

You can have one creation or many, big ones and little ones, finished or in process. Some that you are proud of, some not so much.

We tend to compartmentalize our creations and chop our life up into pieces and parts. This is my job, this is my house, these are my friends, this is my hobby, this is my business. I'm a golfer. I'm a fisherman. I'm an accountant. I'm a hunter. I'm a musician.

But there is a bigger story that often goes untold.

It is easy to be so caught up in day to day living that we don't see the big picture, the most important creation

- the one that brings true happiness, and the one you will work on bringing into being for the rest of your days.

That creation is your life.

When you look at your perfect life as a creation, and decide that you are the force that will bring it into being, then you will understand what dream mountain really is.

Dream mountain is your masterpiece.

And it's not just about things you want, it's also about who you are. My mentor once told me, "If your goal is to have a million dollars, the money isn't nearly as important as who you have to become to get it." Likewise, the most important thing about your dream is who you must become to get it.

Your dream won't happen by accident. You have to make it happen. Making it happen is what grows you. You cannot create what you want by staying the way you are and doing what you are doing. The way you are now is why you have what you have.

If you will pursue it, your dream forces you to become who you are supposed to be. But the power of the dream goes even deeper still, because it's about more than you.

Your life lives on in people you touch, in the lives you change, in the lives of your friends and family, and their friends and family. Every influence you have on another spreads through them to still another. The waves from your creation spread out forever in the universe.

This is how you make it matter that you are here. This is why reality mountain, dream mountain and the trip between them are so important, and why the distance between where you are and what you want is a good thing, not a bad thing.

The distance may feel uncomfortable. It may feel like stress or pain. Maybe it just pisses you off. You can look at it that way if you want to, or you can feel good about it, and recognize that this distance creates the energy that helps you grow into who you are supposed to be.

Let's look at this energy in another way. Imagine two tennis balls attached together by a strong spring. One ball is labeled REALITY, the other as DREAM. Now hold a ball in each hand, move your arms apart, and feel the energy from the spring trying to pull the balls back together. The farther apart they are, the more energy you feel. In physics this is called potential energy, which simply means stored energy. If you let go, that energy is released and the balls fly toward each other.

The distance between the mountains is potential energy too. The distance between what you have and what you want is not a problem to fight against. It is not something to worry and fret about. It is potential energy waiting to help you. The farther away your dream is from your reality, the more potential energy there is in the system.

You have three choices as to how you will close the distance between your reality and your dream.

One choice is to mentally distort your reality to make it appear closer to your dream than it is. In other words lie to yourself. Tell yourself things aren't as bad as they seem, that you don't really want what you want, and use denial, rationalization, excuses. The problem with this choice is that it dooms you to a life of confusion, stress, and mediocrity.

The second choice is to shrink your dream. This a common choice in life, in business, in relationships. It's called copping out - telling yourself to be reasonable, practical, realistic. Kill your own dream. You know the drill. You could even shrink your dream all the way down until it matches your reality. That takes care of the discrepancy doesn't it.

The problem with that choice is that you want what you want. Your dream is in you. If you do not say what you want and move towards it, then conflict lives in you. You won't feel right. You won't have what you were supposed to have, or be who you are supposed to be. Your soul will know this, and you will need to have *that* chat with your soul on your last day. Ouch.

The last choice for decreasing this discrepancy between your reality and your dream is to move your reality towards your dream. This happens when you are honest with yourself about what your true dream is, and then march relentlessly toward it.

This is called creating the life you want.

If the game you are playing is about creating the life you want, then you must anchor your dream in your mind. Do not alter it. Don't waver. Make dream mountain the immovable one.

If you shrink your dream towards your reality, and don't accept the challenge to make your life what it could be and should be, then you are robbing yourself, your loved ones, and the universe of your unique purpose.

Your dream is in you, and to be fulfilled as a human being and give your appropriate contribution to the universe, you have to find it, let it germinate, nurture it, grow it, and share it.

This is how you have a good life. This is how you make your life matter. This is how you create a masterpiece.

Only the painter knows when his painting is complete, and only then will he sign. Your masterpiece will be complete on your last day.

Make it a proud signing.

CHAPTER ELEVEN

Pep Talk

Every person who is good at something started with nothing.

If you have a hobby or something you are good at, you started with nothing too - no skill, no tools, no materials, no knowledge.

Then you got the books, the videos, took the classes, bought some tools, practiced, learned, grew your skills. You paged through the catalogs or searched online longing for the latest gizmo. You spent hours, days, years, or perhaps decades working on your thing.

You didn't bitch all along the way and complain about having to practice and work at it, because it was fun, challenging, and rewarding. Otherwise you wouldn't do it, right?

You enjoyed learning new things, the challenge of getting better at it, buying the things you need or want, practicing, seeing the end result.

Working on your dream can be that way too. Creating the life you want can be your new hobby... if you want it to be.

What if, instead of being stressful and torturous, the trip was an exciting, challenging game with a big prize at the end? It will be that way when you change your mind about what you believe. It is what you think it is.

Unfortunately we grew up with the paradigm that creating a successful life is supposed to be a long, drawn out process. Work hard. Climb the ladder of success one painful rung at a time. Pay your dues. Struggle. Claw your way to a better life.

But it doesn't need to feel like that, nor do you need to be content with incremental or gradual changes. There is no requirement to climb the ladder one rung at a time. You can skip a rung or two. Or throw away the ladder and trampoline to the next level. Instead of going from A to B to C to D, you can go from A to D.

If you've ever driven a stick shift, you know you can only go so fast in 2nd gear, no matter how far down you push the gas pedal or how long you keep it floored. When you hit top speed, your car is doing the best it can in second gear. Don't continue down the highway bitching that your car isn't going fast enough - shift!

It's your turn at bat and the game is on the line. Will you try a safe little blooper to get to first base, or will you swing for the fence? What would happen if you skipped second base and ran straight to third? Yes it's against the rules. Yes people will wonder what's wrong with you. Yes, you "can't" do that. But what if you did? You could play that different kind of game if you wanted to. And the world won't collapse.

Your dream won't happen by thinking the way you always have and doing what you've always done. You know that. You've got to bust out some new moves, break out of your routine, think differently, shift gears, play a different game.

Working harder isn't the answer, because that just means doing more of the things that got you to where you are now. Besides, you are already too busy. How are you going to do more?

Instead do less. Eliminate. Simplify. Get rid of stuff. Throw out mental and physical clutter. Work easier, not harder. Don't do more things, do different things.

Most of all, beware the quicksand trap called doing what you know.

When you try something different with your life, the change comes with feelings of excitement, hope, and exhilaration. Unfortunately, change can also bring fear and doubt - the twin thieves that want to rob you of your future.

In the beginning, your enthusiasm and passion for a better life will overcome the doubts and fears. Somewhere in there though, reality sets in. Things may not be going as smoothly as you thought they would. Doubt takes over - it's not going to work, I can't do this, what was I thinking?

This is the software trying to adjust your thermostat back to where you were. It wants to convince you to go back to your old ways, do what you have always done, do what you know. Shrink you dream, be realistic, accept your position in the world. Stop trying so hard. Settle.

The software knows what buttons to push, all the pretty words to say, and all the justifications and excuses disguised as reasons to go back.

And there you stand... knee deep in quicksand.

This when you must turn to your lists for guidance. If you have done them diligently over and over, the untarnished truth about who you are and what you want is written there, plain as day for all to see. The truth is why you need to proceed forward and not backward.

If you proceed towards your biggest dream, the reality is that you could indeed fail to achieve it. The fear of failure is what keeps many people stuck where they are. But let's think about that.

If you don't try, you don't get your dream. If you try but don't make it, you don't get your dream. Either way the result is the same. But the good news is that there is a valuable consolation prize for trying.

However long or short the trip may be, whether you make it all the way or not, your dream grows you. It makes you better, and prepares you for the next dream. The worst case scenario is that you are a better human, and more able to try again.

At the end, your regrets will not be about the things you did. They will be about the things you didn't do.

Trying something new does not produce regret. Change does not produce regret. Playing a different game does not produce regret.

Regret comes from staying in your rut, from not taking steps you know you need to take, from not trying, from not pursuing your clear and compelling dream.

Real regret comes to visit on the day you realize that you didn't live the life you wanted to, because _____. (fill in the blank).

CHAPTER TWELVE

Interplanetary Games

It's all about you… or is it?

You are the center of your own world called PLANET YOU. Your family, friends, church, workplace, neighborhood, city, state, and country, are all part of your planet.

Everyone else has their planet too, and all the people planets have commonalities and differences. Humans are all the same and all different, and we are all free to feel good or bad about the sameness, or the differences. We are free to find differences interesting, or ugly.

Finding them ugly causes planets to collide. Conflict comes from thinking that other people planets should be like yours, and that you are right and they are wrong. It comes from demanding that others understand you, rather than trying to understand them. Conflict comes from poor communication, ignorance, jealousy, and judgement.

Conflict and bad feelings dissipate when you decide that others mean you no harm, that they do things that make sense to them based on their software, and that like you and I, they are simply in different stages on their trip to dream mountain.

Perhaps the clouds are so thick on reality mountain that they can't see dream mountain. They might be lost in the forest or stuck in the quicksand struggling to survive. Maybe they don't need judgement or harshness, but just a little help instead. And maybe you are the one who will throw them a rope.

If Planet You contains distress, conflict, lack of abundance, anger, resentment, or unhappiness, then healing is needed. Healing comes from getting clear about who you are and what you want, and then taking action.

Your planet will heal as you heal. And as you evolve, so too will your planet and everything in it. As your planet heals and evolves, the people planets surrounding you will be influenced to do likewise.

Improving the world doesn't happen by trying to force others to change. It happens by improving yourself. Everything starts with you.

Fighting, complaining, arguing, and blaming will do nothing. Judging the motivations and actions of others does nothing. This is the game that goes on everywhere all the time - among people, among political parties, among religions, among governments.

Trying to change that game won't help. Stop fighting. Let it be. That game will go on, but you don't need to play anymore. Take your ball and go home. Go play a different game with different rules.

The new game is called FREEDOM, and it starts with you getting on your path to dream mountain, unhindered by all internal and external forces you think are limiting you.

Here are the rules:

Be who you are.

Have what you want.

Do what you love.

Be healthy.

Think how you want to think.

Take responsibility for your life.

Create your circumstances.

Be true to yourself.

Have no concern for what others think of you.

Live according to your values.

Express your unique purpose.

Be prosperous.

Live how you want to live.

Make your unique contribution to the world.

Help others or not as you see fit.

In this game, power and responsibility reside at the level of the individual. In this game you don't need to be taken care of. You don't need to be told what to do, what is acceptable, what you should want, what to think, what you are capable of, or how you should live. Here your planet revolves around your dream, and all the other miscellaneous crap doesn't much matter.

Many people will not like this game because it is built on a framework of personal responsibility. It forces growth and change, and demands that reality be confronted head on. It requires the courage to challenge old thinking and venture down a different path. It asks that the players do more, have more, be more, help more, give more.

Some people won't like any of that. And that's OK. It doesn't mean they are right or wrong, stupid or smart. It just means they can't play here yet.

But for some, it will be right. It will resonate. You feel it when you are in the right game. Your soul feels the congruence between what you believe, who you are, your actions, and the results you see manifested in your life.

As you learn the Game of Freedom and improve your skills, you will begin to understand the wisdom behind the rules and start applying them to everything in your planet. More than that, you will begin to apply them to other people planets as well.

As you respect your time, your freedom, your right to live and think how you want, so too will you respect those things for other people. When you begin treating yourself differently, you will begin treating other people differently. Improving yourself is how you improve your planet, and then other planets, and then perhaps the world.

As you move along your path and struggle to evolve, you may come to realize that your dream is a vehicle to help not just you, but others as well, and that your destiny is to provide your unique contribution to others in the way that is determined by your clear and compelling dream.

Your just rewards for doing so will come in direct proportion to how much help you give others on the path to their dream mountain.

When you give appropriately, you get. The more you give, the more you get. The more you get, the more you can give back. The more you give back, the more you get.

When you have enough, you may choose to give without getting. This is altruism. This is the higher level of being called self-transcendence that sits alone on top of Maslow's hierarchy of needs. This is where following your dream can take you, and this is how you make your life matter at the highest level.

See, ironically, your trip to dream mountain is not really about you, but you have to evolve enough to get to where it isn't. You do that by harnessing the power of your dream. Ultimately and finally, you exist to help others, but you need to put your own oxygen mask on first.

As you evolve, grow, and create abundance, so too will Planet You. Everything in your planet is affected by who you are as a human being. The more your planet serves as a positive influence on the surrounding people planets rather than a source of conflict, the better off the world will be.

But your planet can't grow until you grow.

You are where the rubber meets the road. So stop worrying and fretting about the games being played all around you. Create the discipline to ignore the screeching and discord from the other planets and from the rest of the world, and bring your focus back on what you can do to be a better human.

Trust in the higher power called your dream to guide you in this.

In order to grow and evolve into who you need to be, and to give your appropriate donation to the world, you must have the freedom to be who you are. Only you can give yourself that freedom.

The game is there, waiting for you. The rules are clear. The invitation is open. You can bring your people with you.

Go play.

CHAPTER THIRTEEN

So What

I hope you are a little different than you were before you read this book.

If you are, I hope you're OK with that because you can't go back. You can't put the thoughts back in the box and go back to living unconsciously. You can't hide from reality, and you certainly can't hide from your dream. You may try, but your reality and your dream will peck at you, like chicks trying to break from the egg - relentlessly.

If such is the case, then I'm happy, because I want this book to make a difference in your life, and so do you. That's why you read this far, isn't it? The only way that can happen is if you take concrete actions that cause good changes in your real world. Otherwise it's all just fluff.

Reading a book is just reading a book. It's nothing more than an entertaining distraction unless it spawns change. That's why every thought and concept in this book was laid out carefully, with intention, for the purpose of helping you get the life you want.

And it will happen. But only if you make it happen. You make it happen by reading this book over and over until it sinks in, by doing your exercises, and by taking the next step.

That begs the question, what is the next step? And the answer is always another question - what do you want?

You might not know what you want yet, and that's OK. Figuring it out is a process. Don't expect a lightening bolt epiphany to suddenly show you what you want and what to do next. That epiphany may indeed come, but probably only after you've done your legwork.

Your legwork is thinking deeply, studying yourself, and getting clear about your reality and your dream. It's writing your story and your lists, and rewriting them every day until they gel. It's all part of the struggling and evolving you need to go through on the trip to the dream.

Going to your dream is not about trying to figure everything out ahead of time. It's a learn and adapt as you go process. It's about taking a step before you feel ready, because you will never feel ready.

The reason I put so much emphasis on taking a step is because the only way you are going to figure this out is by moving. Take a step and see if it works. Do something and see how it feels. If it feels good, do it again. If it feels not so good, take another step anyway, and see how that one feels.

If you don't move, nothing happens and there you sit, same as you are now, forever.

If you want a shortcut, here it is. Once you get all the superficial stuff out of the way, you can boil what you want down into just a few things: You want to be healthy, you want to be happy, you want the freedom to be who you are. And you want financial independence, as a tool to give you the others.

Money is a tricky one, because people tend to have deep seated beliefs and strong emotions about money that determine how much of it they have. For now, let's just say money is important like oxygen. You need oxygen to live, but oxygen is not the purpose of life. Likewise you need money, but money is not the purpose.

On the other hand, being free of the need for money gives you more freedom to be who you are. That is why financial freedom is likely near the top of your dream list.

You want money, but you also want to enjoy how you get it. How you spend your time is how you spend your life, and you don't want to spend most of it doing something you hate, for money. You don't want to struggle through the work week just so you can enjoy weekends. You don't want to spend your whole life waiting to enjoy retirement.

What you dream about are days spent bringing your creations to life, doing things you love and are passionate about, playing with hobbies you enjoy. You dream of days where you do what you want - days with no stress, no traffic, no boss to bug you, no office building to trap you. Days full of enthusiasm, optimism, freedom. Saturday morning days.

That's why you want the financial freedom, isn't it? So you can make days like that. You don't want money, you want freedom that money brings you. You want the freedom to have what you want, do what you love, and be who you are.

Your clear and compelling dream is your vision for how you want your life to be. It is the way you will use your unique gifts, talents, and ideas to help others while helping yourself.

Maybe it will be about making changes in your profession, your health habits, your financial habits, or your relationships. Perhaps it means adding new sources of income, volunteering, or restructuring your days to make different use of your time. Maybe it means you will do whatever it takes to create a life filled with days you love.

You've read this book... SO WHAT? Are you going to make it matter? Are you going to do something different? Are you going to take a chance on a new game? Are you going to take a step toward your dream?

If you don't, then your life will simply be another beautiful dream that never happened.

The only way to get the life you want is to create it. You can't copy it, steal it, or buy it. If you don't actively make the choice to create your life, then an accidental life will be created for you by the people around you, and the hodgepodge of software in your head.

If you want an accidental life, then so be it. If you don't, then make a vow to take charge of the software running your life, do the reprogramming you need, and get rid of the toxic viruses, malware, and the toxic people who plant them.

Continue writing and re-writing the story about who you are, what you value, and what you want. Write it down and keep it close to your heart. This is the secret recipe for your happiness cake. This is what gives you honesty and clarity.

These pages are your sanctuary. Turn to them when you are down or confused or stuck in quicksand. Let them be your deep friends. Use them as your map to dream mountain.

Read your sanctuary pages every day, and when you do, feel in your core how it will be when you have the life you want. Generating strong feelings in your mind while thinking about what you want unleashes powerful unseen forces that will help you on your journey. Feel how your life might be different IF...

you focused on possibilities, not limits.

you focused on your dream, not problems.

you didn't box yourself in with perceived boundaries.

you stopped denying what you want.

you didn't limit what you think you can have.

you didn't have problems, just stuff.

your past didn't matter.

your heart believed that you deserve your dream.

your dream is your destiny.

all the boundaries holding you back are imaginary.

Use the power of your dream to expose and change deep seated beliefs, and to determine the choices you make and the actions you take going forward. Do not fear the consequences of your actions, because when you are on the path to your dream, things work out how they are supposed to.

Your dream comes from your soul. It is the only force in the universe that has the power to render everything that is working against you irrelevant. It can make your problems not matter. It can override your belief system, your past, every choice you ever made, and everything that has happened to you so far. All you need do is let it out to play, and remember that dreams require action.

Don't try to plan every step to dream mountain ahead of time. You can't know all the steps ahead of time anyway, nor do you need to. You only need to know the next one.

If taking a big step feels right, then do it. If a baby step feels right, do that. Then take another one every day. It doesn't matter what the step is, only that you take it.

Your dream is waiting...

Epilogue:
A Perfect Storm

Dream mountain is waiting for you.

The question is, how are you going to get there? You might have your dream in your mind and your perfectly possible days laid out on paper. You've got your lists of who you are and what you want.

But you need to bring those things to life.

When you use the power of reality mountain, dream mountain, and the potential energy between them properly, the how will happen - but only if you let it happen.

There is an old parable about a guy stranded on his rooftop in a raging flood. Being the religious guy he was, he just knew God was going to save him, so when people came by in a canoe and offered him a ride, he politely refused, saying "God will save me!" When a power boat came by, he refused again, saying "God will save me!" Finally, a helicopter hovered overhead with people imploring him to grab the rope and be hoisted on board. He refused again, saying "I'm waiting for God to save me!"

Finally he was swept off the roof and drowned. When he got to heaven, he said to God, "I am so disappointed in you. I had the faith. I believed you would save me. Why did you leave me to die?"

God looked at him quizzically and said, "I sent a canoe, a power boat, and a helicopter to save you. What more were you waiting for?"

When the how shows up in your life, pay attention, be aware, make your move. When your canoe comes by, don't sit on your rooftop waiting for whatever it is you think you are waiting for.

Many people remain frozen where they are because of fear, doubt, and confusion about what they want and what to do next. Many have difficulty seeing a path to their preferred future.

I don't want that to be you, and I don't want to leave you hanging without a next step - so I have designed one for you.

Your clear and compelling dream is about creating the life you want. If not now, then someday it will also be about using your unique gifts to help others and make the world a better place. It will be about making your life matter.

You have the hobbies, passions, and creations you love. You have unique gifts. Your happiness lies where your gifts and passions intersect with the needs of people who want what you have to give.

If you can find a way to provide value to others by doing what you are passionate about, then you will receive appropriate rewards, and be on your way to adding more and more perfectly possible days to your life.

What if you could dream about a life where you create more income or even financial freedom by doing things you love and being who you are? What if you could turn your hobbies or your passions into what you do much of the time?

That may seem like a pipe dream, and for most people, for most of history, it was. It isn't anymore.

The world tends to plod along, evolving and growing slowly. Then every once in awhile, when conditions are right, it takes a quantum leap ahead. It happened with the invention of the steam engine, television, and the automobile for example. Most recently, the era of the computer literally changed the entire world.

And now, the computer age has led to the dawn of a new era. Powerful forces are converging to create opportunities for personal advancement that never existed before. A perfect storm of possibility is here.

I am excited about this storm because I've spent the last ten years working on ways to create freedom using technology. It's always been possible for the select few with the skills to pull it off, but now it's finally a possibility for most people, regardless of education, skills, or knowledge.

It's possible because internet technology has finally evolved to where an average person can create a structure, a system, a mechanism to bring their dream into existence.

This is especially amazing because you don't even need to know what your dream is yet. If you are confused about your dream, you can create the structure first, then try different things, test ideas, plug a potential dream in, and see what happens. The system allows you to experiment and evolve into your dream.

There has never been a better time in history to turn your dream into reality, and create a life you truly enjoy.

If you would like to see how this is possible, I've created a possible next step on the path to your clear and compelling dream. Simply go to mikepierquet.com/book-bonus and check out the videos you will find there.

The first is about a simple, effective tool I use to guide my own life. I call it the Dreamer Diamond. It is a matrix that provides a quick, easy way to help you define and focus on exactly what matters to you in each area of your life. It will help you think through what it is that you really want. This one video can change a lot of things for you.

You will also find videos that explain the perfect storm, and lay out step by step how you can create a structure to bring your dream into existence - starting today.

The bonuses are free. There is no catch. I think you will like them. Check them out and see if anything resonates.

If you feel like an evolving kind of person, and would like to hang with similar critters, I invite you to visit my website at **mikepierquet.com.**

If you have comments about this book, please email them to me at **support@mikepierquet.com**. If you will send me a testimonial about the book, I will send you a surprise gift.

If you would like additional copies of this book for your friends, family, and business associates, you can find some at **clearandcompellingdream.com**

Thank you very much for reading my book. I hope it made at least a little difference in your life. Good luck on your journey, and I hope to see you somewhere along the path.

About The Author

Michael Pierquet is a free thinker who lives a simple, clutter free life with his dog Jesse and a few material possessions. His hobby is being on the beach at sunrise, writing and thinking. His mission is helping people grow better lives.

(also entrepreneur, photographer, dentist, and evolving human being).

www.ingramcontent.com/pod-product-compliance
Lightning Source LLC
Chambersburg PA
CBHW021843090426
42811CB00033B/2119/J

9780982793718